Sitting Bull

![Cherry Lake Press logo] CHERRY LAKE PRESS

Published in the United States of America by Cherry Lake Publishing Group
Ann Arbor, Michigan
www.cherrylakepublishing.com

Reading Adviser: Beth Walker Gambro, MS, Ed., Reading Consultant, Yorkville, IL
Book Designer: Jennifer Wahi
Illustrator: Jeff Bane

Photo Credits: © Public Domain/Internet Archive Book Images/flickr, 5; © Kris Wiktor/Shuttershock, 7; © Public Domain/Heritage Auctions/Wikimedia, 9; © Public Domain/Internet Archive Book Images/flickr, 11; © Library of Congress/Photograph by D. F. Barry/LOC No. 95522828, 13, 22; © Phawat/Shuttershock, 15; © Public Domain/Saskatchewan Archives/Wikimedia, 17; © Library of Congress/Photograph by D.F. Barry/LOC No. 2007675831, 19, 23; © Library of Congress/Photograph by D. F. Barry/LOC No. 94506170, 21; Cover, 1, 12, 14, 18, Jeff Bane; Various frames throughout, © Shutterstock Images

Cherry Lake Press is an imprint of Cherry Lake Publishing Group.

Library of Congress Cataloging-in-Publication Data

Names: Thiele, June, author. | Bane, Jeff, 1957- illustrator.
Title: Sitting Bull / by June Thiele ; illustrator, Jeff Bane.
Description: Ann Arbor, Michigan : Cherry Lake Publishing, [2023] | Series: My itty-bitty bio
Identifiers: LCCN 2022009910 | ISBN 9781668908907 (hardcover) | ISBN 9781668910504 (paperback) | ISBN 9781668912096 (ebook) | ISBN 9781668913680 (pdf)
Subjects: LCSH: Sitting Bull, 1831-1890--Juvenile literature. | Dakota Indians--Biography--Juvenile literature. | Hunkpapa Indians--Biography--Juvenile literature.
Classification: LCC E99.D1 T45 2023 | DDC 978.004/9752440092 [B]--dc23/eng/20220321
LC record available at https://lccn.loc.gov/2022009910

Printed in the United States of America
Corporate Graphics

About the author: June Thiele writes and acts in Chicago where they live with their wife and child. June is Dena'ina Athabascan and Yup'ik, Indigenous cultures of Alaska. They try to get back home to Alaska as much as possible.

About the illustrator: Jeff Bane and his two business partners own a studio along the American River in Folsom, California, home of the 1849 Gold Rush. When Jeff's not sketching or illustrating for clients, he's either swimming or kayaking in the river to relax.

I was born in South Dakota in 1831. I became a **Lakota** warrior at 14 years old. My **tribe** said I was fearless.

I led a group of warriors. I helped expand our hunting grounds.

I fought against the U.S. Army.
I did this for the first time in 1863.
The army accused my people.
They said we did something.
But we didn't.

I inspired my people. They saw my bravery. I became **chief** of my tribe.

Who inspires you?

I wanted peace for my people. We agreed to sign a **treaty** with the United States. This treaty promised land for my people.

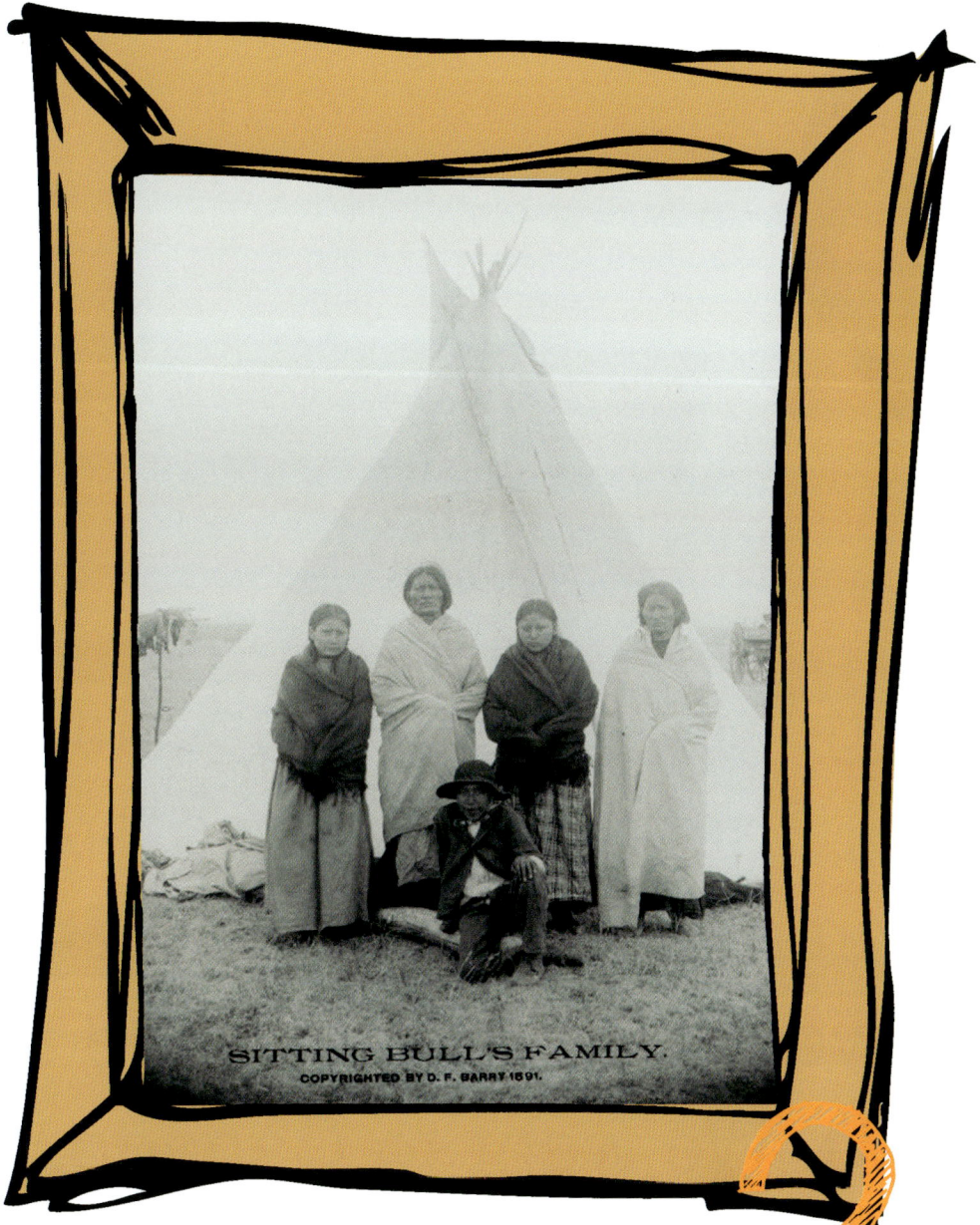

SITTING BULL'S FAMILY.
COPYRIGHTED BY D. F. BARRY 1891.

What is something you want?

But gold was found on our land. The United States broke the treaty. I fought back. But we were eventually forced to move. We went to Canada.

But Canada refused us. We were forced to return to the United States. I was **captured** but later released.

I joined a **Wild West show**.
I became famous. Other **Native Americans** soon joined the show.
It started a movement.

I was killed in 1890. But my **legacy** lives on. I am known for being brave and strong. I am remembered by my people.

What would you like to ask me?

1868

1830

↑
Born
1831

1885

1930

Died
1890

glossary

captured (KAP-churd) took by force

chief (CHEEF) a leader of a tribal community or a clan

Lakota (luh-KOH-tuh) a Native American tribe located in South Dakota; subculture of the Sioux people

legacy (LEH-guh-see) something handed down from one generation to another

Native Americans (NAY-tiv uh-MER-uh-kuhnz) people who originally lived in America, or relatives of these people

treaty (TREE-tee) a formal promise

tribe (TRYB) a group of people including many families, clans, or generations

Wild West show (WYLD WEST SHOH) a traveling show that included horseback riding, shooting contests, and other skills

index